Color the Psalms

Artwork by Michal Sparks

HARVEST HOUSE PUBLISHERS
EUGENE, OREGON

Design and production by Harvest House Publishers Inc.

COLOR THE PSALMS

Copyright © 2016 by Michal Sparks
Published by Harvest House Publishers
Eugene, Oregon 97402
www.harvesthousepublishers.com

ISBN 978-0-7369-6790-7 (pbk.)

Printed in United States of America

15 16 17 18 19 20 21 22 23 / VP-JH / 10 9 8 7 6 5 4 3 2 1

A Good Place to Begin

This coloring book is for artists of all ages and talents, and that means you! Let your creative spirit free, choose any color you like, and make each beautiful image your own. There are no rules except to have fun.

Enjoy the process. Feel free to use colored pencils, pens, water colors, markers, and crayons—or any combination thereof—to add color and texture to each design. Notice that all the pictures are printed on just one side of the paper. To keep colors from bleeding through to the next page, simply slip an extra piece of paper underneath the page you're working on. When finished, you might like to cut the page from the book, trim it to size, and frame your artwork for all to see.

Most importantly, have fun with the process. Enjoy experimenting with contrasting colors or different shades of the same color. Try lighter hues for a softer look or layer and blend your colors for even more options. Allow some white space or saturate the entire piece with rich vibrant color, depending on your mood. Let your worries go, relax in the moment, and allow your creative spirit to lead the way!

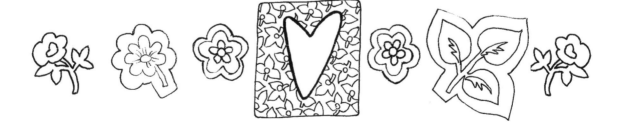

You will show me
the path of life;
In Your presence is
fullness of joy;
At Your right hand are
pleasures
forevermore.

PSALM 16:11

The Lord has done great things for us.

Psalm 126:3

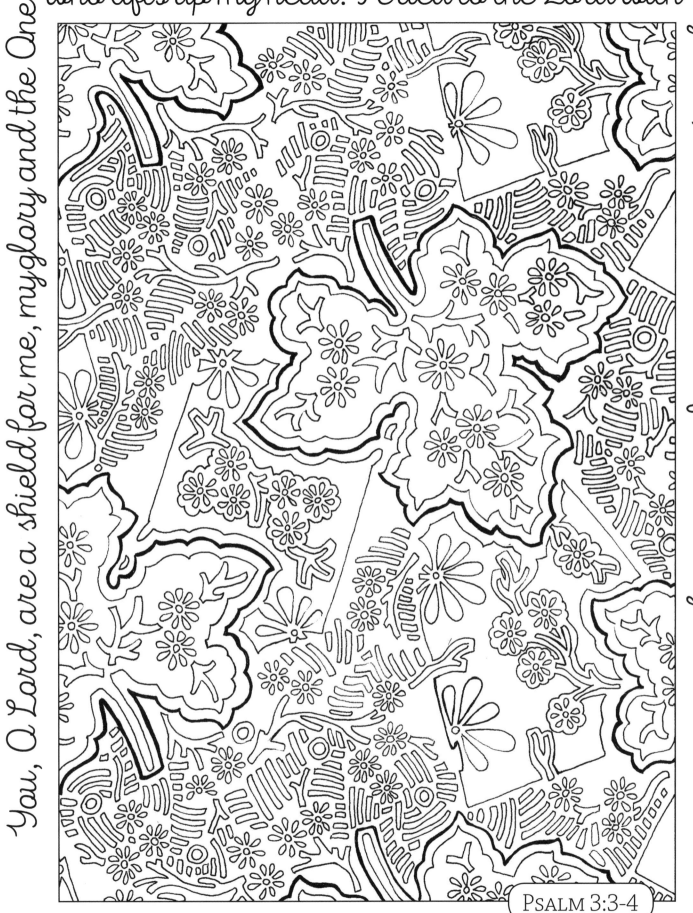

who lifts up my head. I cried to the Lord with my voice, and He heard me from His holy hill.

You, O Lord, are a shield for me, my glory, and the One

Psalm 3:3-4

The earth is the Lord's,
and all its fullness,
the world and those who
dwell therein.

PSALM 24:1

Psalm 37:3

I sought the Lord, and

He heard me,

and delivered me

from all my fears.

PSALM 34:4

He is our help and our shield.

PSALM 33:20

He makes me to lie down in green pastures;

The Lord is my shepherd; I shall not want.

He leads me beside the still waters. He restores my soul.

Psalm 23:1-3

The Lord is near to those
who have a *broken heart*,
and saves such as have a
contrite spirit.

Psalm 34:18

He hears my voice & my prayer for Mercy.

PSALM 116:1

The heavens declare
the glory of God;
And the firmament shows
His handiwork.

PSALM 19:1

PSALM 23:1

who made heaven and earth.

Your word

is a lamp to my feet and
a light to my path.

Psalm 119:105

He alone is my rock and my Salvation.

PSALM 62:2

Restore to me the
joy of Your salvation,
and uphold me by
Your generous Spirit.

Psalm 51:12

The LORD is my light and my Salvation

Psalm 27:1

mercy shall follow me all the days of my life; And I will dwell in the house of the Lord forever.

My cup runs over. Surely goodness and

Psalm 23:5-6

Delight yourself
also in the Lord,
and He shall give you
the desires of your heart.

PSALM 37:4

Be still and know that I am God

Psalm 46:10

Yea, though I walk
through the valley of
the shadow of death,
I will fear no evil;
For You are with me;
Your rod and Your staff,
they comfort me.

Psalm 23:4

I lift up my eyes to the hills... my help comes from the Lord.

Psalm 121:1,2

I will praise You,
for I am *fearfully* and
wonderfully made;
Marvelous are Your works,
and that my soul
knows very well.

PSALM 139:14

Create a pure ♥ in me O GOD

Psalm 51:10

Do not withhold Your tender mercies from me, O Lord; Let Your lovingkindness and Your truth continually preserve me.

Psalm 40:11

Teach me to
do Your will,

for You are my God;
Your Spirit is good.

Lead me in the land
of uprightness.

Psalm 143:10

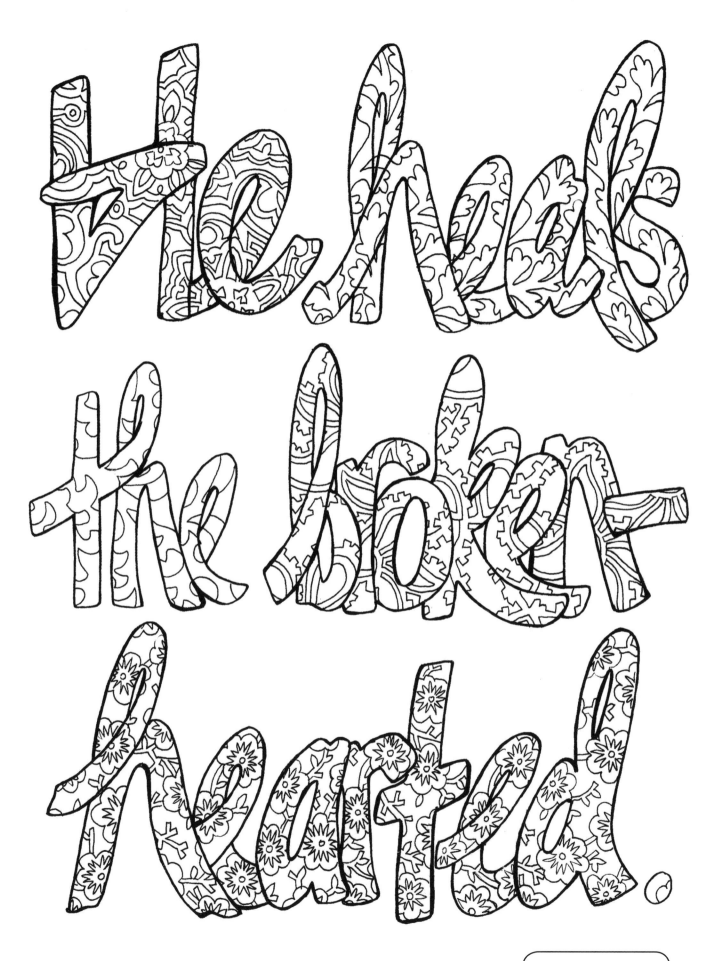

He heals the broken hearted.

PSALM 147:3

Cast your burden
on the Lord, and
He shall sustain you;
He shall never permit
the righteous to be moved.

PSALM 55:22

Psalm 33:20

God is our refuge and strength,

a very present help in trouble.

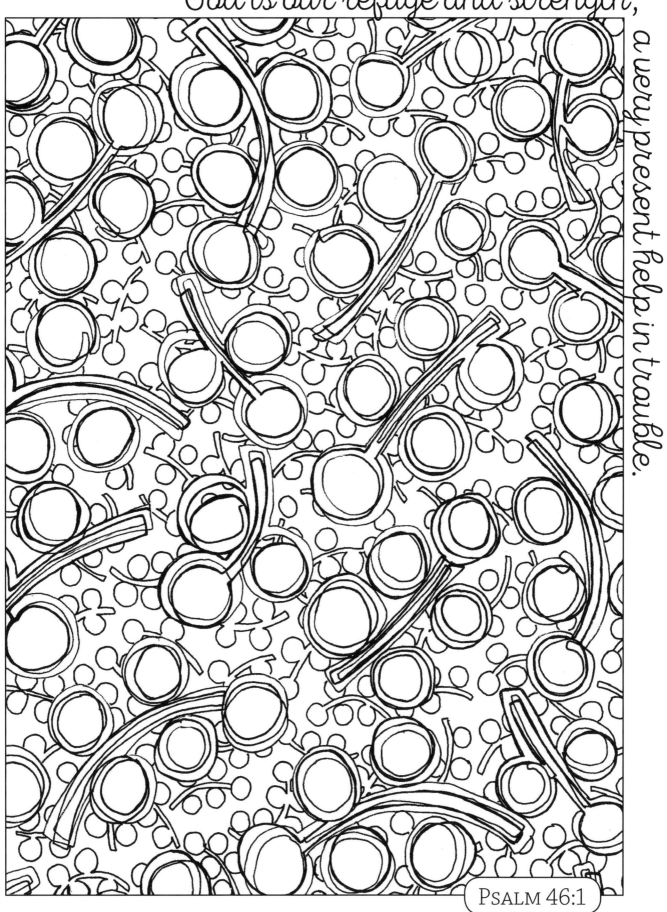

Psalm 46:1

When my heart is
overwhelmed;
Lead me to the rock
that is higher than I.

PSALM 61:2

Under His wings you shall take refuge.

PSALM 91:4

Give thanks to the Lord, **for He is good!** For His mercy endures forever.

PSALM 107:1

His greatness is unsearchable. One generation

Great is the Lord, and greatly to be praised; And

shall praise. Your works to another.

Psalm 145:3-4

This is the day
the Lord has made;
We will rejoice and
be glad in it.

PSALM 118:24

O Lord, my Strength & my Redeemer.

Psalm 19:14

will give grace and glory; No good thing will

He withhold from those who walk uprightly.

For the Lord God is a sun and shield; the Lord

Psalm 84:11

Michal Sparks's artwork can be found throughout the home-furnishings industry in textiles, gift items, dinnerware, and more. She is the artist for *Words of Comfort for Times of Loss* and *When Someone You Love Has Cancer*. She and her family live in New Jersey.

For more information on more
Harvest House coloring books for adults, go to
www.harvesthousepublishers.com.